THE PUMPKIN KING

This is
BIG PUMPKIN Country
Brenda J. Patterson 79
Grown
438 1/2
WE GROW PUMPKINS LIKE
FOR THE ATLANTIC PUMPK
OCT. 7-14

THE
PUMPKIN KING

Howard Dill
and the Atlantic Giant

by
Al Kingsbury

LANCELOT PRESS
HANTSPORT, NOVA SCOTIA

On the front cover:
Howard poses with Joshua Dill and a championship specimen.
(Shirley Spencer)
On the back cover:
Kristin Phillips brings a jack-o'-lantern to life in the Dill pumpkin
patch. (Michael Melford)
On the frontispiece:
Dill won his first international championship at Philadelphia in
1979 with a 438.5-pound entry. (Hutten)

Acknowledgements:
Thanks to *The Chronicle-Herald* and the *Hants Journal* for use of
photos and news files in compiling the information for this book.

ISBN 0-88999-516-8
Published 1992
    Fifth printing 1995
Revised edition printed March 1996

Printed on recycled acid-free paper
Book design by Doug Porter
Cover design by Doug Pope

LANCELOT PRESS LIMITED
Hantsport, Nova Scotia. Office and production facilities located on
Hwy. 1, 1/2 mile east of Hantsport.

Mailing address:
P.O. Box 425, Hantsport, Nova Scotia B0P 1P0

TABLE OF CONTENTS

Howard Dill. (Fairclough Studio)

THE BELOVED HOWARD DILL

by Peter J. & Nancy G. Rigoloso

Howard Dill IS singularly the most important person in the world of championship pumpkin growing. If it were not for this remarkable, soft spoken man, the World Pumpkin Confederation would have little upon which to base its existence. Howard is part and parcel of our raison d'etre (our reason for being). Without Howard's Atlantic Giant, the variety which took him most of his lifetime to breed, giant pumpkin aficionados around the world would be struggling to grow 200 pound specimens, considering themselves lucky if they were able to do that.

We are fortunate, indeed, that it was Howard who developed the Atlantic Giant we use in our mighty pursuits. If we have received national and international acclaim for our mastery as pumpkin growers and gardeners, then we are constrained to confess the name of Howard Dill to one and all.

The fact that Howard is the only individual to be jointly honored with the World Pumpkin Confederation's highest tribute, the Lifetime Service and Achievement Award, and simultaneously inducted into our Hall of Fame, was no accident. This was a contrived, deliberate action designed to permanently set Howard apart from the rest of us for the sake of history. It was meant to give to him an honor that will remain, for all practical purposes, an unachievable prize; it is unlikely that the two awards will ever be given to an individual in the same year again. Howard Dill, four times in succession World Champion, is unquestionably the Babe Ruth of pumpkin growers, the Sultan of Squash, the King of Cucurbits. We crown him the Reigning Monarch of Landwhalers: Moby Dill.

There are noble characteristics of great men we esteem that strike us to the core and, no matter how muddled our lives may be, we are inspired to pay witness to them: humility, compassion, honesty, charity and wisdom are among the virtues we hold most dear. These words are the expressions of integrity we are compelled to apply to one of the finest men it has ever been our privilege to know. These are the expressions people use to raise up, shoulder high, the best of us – the words that write down Howard Dill, the Atlantic Giant.

Where do such men come from and why do we love them so? Their lives are a gift of the heart, an offering of the spirit. These rare individuals remind us that we can be greater than ourselves. Their honor is public property, their achievement is our glory. Special people, like Howard Dill, represent Everyman. Howard has always been there for us, offering kind words of encouragement, and because he does not forget us, we will not forget him. For all that he has given of himself to others, for so many years, the World Pumpkin Confederation has bestowed upon him this recognition~ offering Howard our appreciation of his worthiness of praise, for, truly, people like Howard Dill are a light to the world.

Howard, on behalf of your multitude of friends worldwide, we say to you the words that are rightfully yours. You are a great man, revered and cherished in our hearts. You have earned the right to live within us, and for your graciousness, kindness, and humanity you will live within the hearts of all who love the light and shun the darkness. The impact of your life, long after you have passed, will remain alive in the spirit that drives mankind to decency, compassion and brotherhood. The footprints of your life will not be washed away by water, blown away by wind, or erased from our memory by time. God bless you for what you have given us and what you will give future generations. And with people like you, Howard, the best is yet to come!

CHAPTER ONE

FROM CINDERELLA

TO HOWARD DILL

FROM THE TIME that Cinderella's fairy godmother first waved her magic wand in the centuries-old fairytale, giant pumpkins have been a part of the world's folklore and fascination.

Perhaps it's because they are by nature the largest of fruits, and command attention in any display.

Or maybe it has something to do with their brilliant color.

Or perhaps a combination of the two.

Whatever the reason, big pumpkins have intrigued generations, both in folklore and real life. Jack's beanstalk has been the only substantial rival for prolific growth and fantasy.

Giant pumpkins have been the subject of legends through the centuries and in recent years have found their way into comic strips.

The big pumpkin which the fairy godmother transformed into a golden coach for Cinderella has continued to be the best known of all, but there have been others which have captured our imagination and been the subject of tall tales.

Ellen Fergusson visits with a scarecrow relaxing amidst an assortment of pumpkins at the Dill farm. (Spencer)

Cinderella's seems to be the only one that has provided transportation, but several have been used for shelter.

Like the one in the nursery rhyme:

> Peter, Peter, pumpkin eater
> Had a wife and couldn't keep her;
> He put her in a pumpkin shell,
> And there he kept her very well.

In a legend of India, a devoted father used a huge pumpkin as a tomb for his only son. In time, the pumpkin was found to be filled with fish. In an attempt to take the fish, four brothers tried to carry the pumpkin away but became frightened and dropped it. A flood of water poured out of the cracked shell, inundating the earth.

America gave the pumpkin a special place in its folklore

by associating it with the celebration of Thanksgiving and in the *Legend of Sleepy Hollow*. In that classic, the Headless Horseman lifts his pumpkin head from the pommel of his saddle and hurls it at the fleeing Ichabod Crane.

Pumpkins have a special place in Hallowe'en celebrations when they are hollowed out for use as jack-o'-lanterns.

That custom goes back to early England, when an order of Celtic priests, called Druids, burned fires to ward off evil spirits.

During the Middle Ages, the Irish thought that pale swamp fires they saw rising over marshes as swamp gas spontaneously ignited on damp evenings were the wandering souls of the dead.

To ward off the wicked spirits, they hollowed out potatoes and turnips, inserted tiny candles to form lanterns and placed them in the window on All Hallow's Eve.

To round out the custom, they created the *Tale of Jack*. It tells of a homeless soul who couldn't get into Heaven because he was stingy and wasn't allowed into Hell, because he tried to trick the devil. The tale continues as Jack searches for the rest he would never find.

The Irish brought their *Tale of Jack* to America and continued the tradition of gathering on October 31 to tell ghost stories and sing songs. The settlers adapted their potato and turnip carving traditions to fit the American pumpkin.

Shakespeare refers to the pumpkin in *Merry Wives of Windsor* as a "gross, watery pumpion," and other stories focus on the prolific growth of pumpkin vines.

There's the legend of the youth named Jack who mounted his horse one spring to plant pumpkins. As he dropped seed in prepared hills, he spurred his mount at top speed, but still was unable to keep ahead of the fast-growing vines.

The *Old Farmer's Almanac* of 1966 recalled the tale of the Racer Pumpkin of 1763. That prolific plant is said to have sent its vines across the Connecticut River into the town of Vernon, Vermont. A sow from the farm where the pumpkin was planted disappeared in the fall and apparently scampered across the river on the vine. She was found the following spring, living inside a huge Racer Pumpkin, which had sheltered and fed her and her 101 babies all winter.

Pumpkins have no less a fascination today.

In an elaborate, annual fall ceremony at University of New Brunswick in Canada, residents of Harrison House carry out the Ceremonial Sacrifice of the Great Pumpkin. A huge pumpkin is carried on a litter to the courtyard of Lady Dunn Hall, where it is blessed and illuminated. It is then taken to the roof of the Upper Lounge, from where, following more ceremony, it is hurled to the ground, bursting in a pillar of flame. Spectators then toss their candles into the burning remains before heading to the bar for pumpkin punch and festive celebrations.

Cartoonist Charles Schulz brought the fascination for pumpkins to a whole new generation in his *Peanuts* comic strip. He has Linus begin a never-ending search for the Great Pumpkin, which will bring candy for all the children.

In real life, a few individuals have made attempts over the years to develop and grow the great pumpkin, but only one has had consistent success and he has been acknowledged as the world's Pumpkin King.

Canadian farmer Howard Dill, who operates a small farm in Windsor, Nova Scotia, has developed a variety of pumpkin seeds called Dill's Atlantic Giant. His seeds have enabled him to claim the title for growing the world's heaviest pumpkin in four successive years and other growers have used his seeds to set world records over the past decade.

Jack-o'-lanterns have long been a part of Hallowe'en lore. (Melford)

Donald Mullen admires a Thanksgiving display of Atlantic Giants at
New Tusket Baptist Church in Yarmouth County, N.S.

He has his own philosophy on the pumpkin's lure.

"Giant pumpkins get people out and take them away
from the world's bad news.

"There's something about pumpkins, especially when
they're big, that makes people happy. The bigger the
pumpkin, the happier it seems to make them feel. If they see
one at an exhibition, it gives them a day to get all the bad
things off their minds.

"It plays a vital role in more ways than one. What else
can you grow that has the power to make people happy?"

CHAPTER TWO

PASTIME TO

PASSION

IT'S A SMALL FAMILY farm on College Road in Windsor, Nova Scotia, which produced not just the world's heaviest pumpkins for four successive years, but also the Pumpkin King himself.

The homestead was built in the 19th century by Alexander Dill. When he moved to Massachusetts, it was taken over by John Dill and then passed down through successive generations to Fred Dill and William Dill.

When William and Gladys Dill ran the farm during the 1930s to 1950s era, it consisted of a small fruit orchard, market garden and a fairly large dairy herd. It was there that they raised their family of three children, Maxine, Margaret and Howard.

Howard Dill, born July 22, 1934, recalls that there was not much time for childhood relaxation or pleasure, as there were many chores to be done, including milking the cows by hand.

"However, like many young boys growing up in that kind of environment, one seems to develop an interest in one or more things. In my case, school was not one of them, as my father believed the farm should come first."

During those early years in Howard's life, economic times were hard. The Second World War was being fought and everyone felt the effects of rationing and trying to bear the costs of war.

He recalls that, "Times became even harder for my father and family after the war, when we lost our mother in June of 1947. She died of tuberculosis, at the age of 43."

This was a severe blow to all, especially the children, who then had to pitch in considerably more with house and barn chores, along with attending school, which was over a mile away. In those days, they walked to school and came home at noon for lunch, even in winter, making a total of four miles to walk every day.

Howard recalls that, "In the winter months, my father would have to keep the fires going in both kitchen and furnace, along with preparing something for lunch at noontime. This was in addition to all the barn chores, milking cows and tending to a great number of laying hens, which supplied 30 to 60 dozen eggs per week to the local hospital, as well as customers in town.

"My sister Margaret quickly learned to cook and was a big help in running the house. That also involved washing milk buckets and cans, as my older sister Maxine was finishing high school and preparing for a business course. Our neighbours, however, were very good through those early, difficult times, by bringing food and helping in other ways."

On winter evenings, the elder Dill would often tell stories about the great hockey teams and players of the past and present eras. Young Howard quickly became a great student of those handed-down stories and turned his attention to collecting photos and programs of NHL teams during the 1940s. That pastime has not only continued, but has become a passion second only to his obsession for

Andrew and Diana Dill share their father's pride as he weighed the international champion 493.5-pounder that held the world record for four years. (Kingsbury)

Howard Dill, right, with rival grower Owen Woodman of Falmouth, at a Hants County Exhibition contest. (Hants Journal)

growing giant pumpkins.

William Dill (or Dick as he was better known) also was a great supporter of agricultural exhibitions and every year he took his family across town to North America's oldest agricultural fair. There he would show a few of his better Guernsey cattle, along with vegetables.

Howard soon became involved with the 4-H program and would enter his own calf each fall at the local fair and at other exhibitions around the province.

Of all the items his father entered in the exhibitions each year, Howard noticed that it was the giant pumpkins which always seemed to attract a lot of attention and conversation.

Local competition in those days was almost entirely a Dill family affair, with many of the farming cousins vying for bragging rights. These included John and Joseph Dill and, in later years, William's brother-in-law, Gordon Dill. Other local farmers, including Bill McNeil and Irvin Sandford, always were strong competitors at the Windsor exhibition.

"The competition seemed to impress me even when my father would quite often lose a contest to farming friends or relatives by five or 10 pounds," Howard recalls.

"Although pumpkins back then would normally weigh around the 75- to 80-pound range, they looked big to me."

Those weights continued to stand for years, until Howard became involved in the farming operations and particularly the care of the giant pumpkins.

Although he had no formal education or background in genetics or breeding techniques, the young farmer began devoting more time each year to trying to grow a bigger and better pumpkin to show at the Hants County Exhibition.

"Each season I would look at the different features of the pumpkin my father had been growing and notice different traits that would help in my breeding program. After examining the characteristics of several pumpkins, I noticed likes and dislikes that I would set my sights on in my quest to develop a much larger pumpkin. These features would include factors such as wall thickness, length, height and color."

As the seasons passed, he discovered that giant pumpkin growing was a very creative, educational enjoyment and pastime, as weights were beginning to increase each year under special cultural practices and attention.

It was not until the 1960s, though, that things really started to happen in the Dill pumpkin patch. He topped the 100-pound mark in 1967 and in two years' time was growing 200-pounders.

Although he was continuing to move towards his goal of producing a real giant, Dill admits that he had no more technical expertise than when he started out.

"From a horticultural and technical standpoint, I had absolutely no idea of what I was doing, but I felt that whatever I was doing, it was right."

It was at that point he felt the time had come to explore the world of giant pumpkins further, to see what information was available about growing techniques and previous weights from other competitions abroad.

After obtaining a great deal of research material from departments of agriculture in both Canada and the United States, he discovered that he was a long way from the big leagues of giant pumpkin and squash growing.

He learned that another Nova Scotian, Charles Hewitt of Lunenburg County, held the world record for pumpkins, set at 229 pounds at the old Halifax Dominion Exhibition in 1883. The largest pumpkin ever grown in the United States was produced by Joseph Dunn of Bryantsville, Kentucky, in 1884. It weighed 226 pounds. In the squash category, Hewitt also held the world record of 292 pounds, set in 1883.

His research also showed that William Warnock of Goderich, Ontario, had grown a series of giant pumpkins which peaked at the specimen weighing 403 pounds and was shown at the St. Louis World's Fair in 1903.

These humbling revelations soon showed the Windsor upstart that he had a long way to go to top the previous international records.

After reading Warnock's directions for growing giant

Federal agriculture department employee Bill Lang weighs
one of Dill's early giants, considered a whopper then
at 287.5 pounds. (Elliott)

pumpkins, Dill was inspired to challenge his outstanding records.

Dill had good reason to believe that the seed his father had been using had come from the now-defunct Rennie Seed Company in Ontario, whose seed catalogue could be found in just about every gardener's and farmer's home in Canada in those early years of the century.

Rennie's had purchased Warnock's prize specimen in 1904 for just $10.00 and then sold its seeds at three for 25

Even a 165-pound squash dwarfed Dill's son Danny, who was about six years old at the time. (Spencer)

cents.

Dill realized the genetic potential of the seed when making the right crosses between the Goderich Giant and Genuine Mammoth, another variety his father had been growing between the 1920s and '50s.

During the '50s and '60s, Dill began a self-managed selection process, using the family seed stock. Hand pollination and selection techniques were practised and recorded until 1973, when it became apparent to him that two strains were isolated.

One was producing mature fruit which was long and wide and the other a more globular and uniform fruit. Dill began to concentrate on the more upright of the two, while keeping both in experimentation.

He explains that in order to control self- and cross-pollination, it is necessary to hand pollinate with certain male staminate flowers on certain female pistillate flowers to produce the desired seed. Sometimes pollen of one species is capable of causing seedless fruits to set from staminate flowers of another plant or species.

The giant pumpkin family (genus Cucurbita C. Maxima) contains a large assortment of plant characteristics which offer the possibility of new combinations for bigger and better pumpkins. As this genetic variability has developed, however, crossing the related plants of the pumpkin family can become more difficult.

American horticulturist Ashby M. Rhodes explained in an Illinois research publication in 1951 that "breeding giant pumpkins can be compared to a game of cards, in which Mother Nature has made the rules and dealt out the hands.

"The genes found in Cucurbita may be considered the deck of cards. Real cards are recognized by their suit and number or picture. Genes cannot be seen, but are recognized by their efforts on individual characters, especially in the seed and peduncle (fruit stem).

"Just as certain combinations of cards produce a winning hand, so do certain combinations of genes survive as species.

"Rules of a card prevent us from exchanging cards from one hand to another after the cards have been dealt. The exchange of genes by crossing some species is prevented by sterility barriers that have arisen during the course of evolution.

"But if we can't exchange cards, we can sometimes redeal them to get a new and possibly better hand. Before redealing, all hands are put back in the deck and reshuffled.

"Can we redeal genes to get a new species or perhaps improve an old one?"

For the next number of years, Dill continued his seed selection and target breeding techniques, along with trying different cultural practices that were so important to consistently grow enormous-sized pumpkins.

The secret to success at this point was choosing the proper site, soil preparations and special seed which had built-in genetic traits for super size.

By 1977, his new standard open-pollination variety appeared to be quite stable and by the early '80s, he decided it was time to apply for plant variety protection for the seed he had named Dill's Atlantic Giant. The name was chosen to honor its origins in the Atlantic seacoast province of Nova Scotia.

As Dill continued to make progress in developing his seeds, he and others pushed them to ever-greater limits through international weighoff competitions.

By 1984, the amateur breeder had won four consecutive world championships and held the world record of 493.5 pounds. His seed had proven itself, but not even Dill could yet realize its full potential.

Howard Dill watches intently as Agriculture Canada inspector Rex
Peach weighs the 1980 winner at the Atlantic Winter Fair in
Windsor. The old platform scale registered the weight as
448 pounds, but a few days later the pumpkin was weighed at 459
pounds at Philadelphia. (Kingsbury)

Giant pumpkin growing was now becoming
increasingly popular with gardeners on several continents
and demand for seed was coming from growers and seed
companies around the world.

Dill contracted with Hollar and Company of Colorado
and Western Hybrids Seed Company in California to
reproduce Atlantic Giant seeds in volume to meet the
demand.

The Burgess Seed Company, which was located in
Michigan but has since moved to Bloomington, Illinois, was

Stan Riggs and his daughter Erica, Cambridge, Kings County, N.S., play ring-around-a pumpkin with their first-place entry of 394 pounds in the 1986 Windsor Pumpkin Festival. (Kingsbury)

the first American firm to feature the Atlantic Giant, while the Vesey Seed Company of York, Prince Edward Island, led the way in introduction of the Show King squash, another variety developed at the Dill farm.

CHAPTER THREE

INTERNATIONAL

COMPETITION

INTERNATIONAL competition in the sport of giant pumpkin growing dates back to at least 1893. It was that year that the late William Warnock of Goderich, Ontario, set the record of 365 pounds at the Chicago World's Fair.

Warnock was back in world competition again in 1900, at the World's Fair in Paris, this time weighing in with a specimen of 400 pounds and winning a bronze medal from the French government.

To cap his winning ways and international championships, he boosted his record weight to 403 pounds with an entry in the St. Louis World's Fair three years later.

Interest by Canadians in international competition appears to have waned after that, or at least kept a low profile for many decades.

It was the CBC radio program *As It Happens* that finally stirred interest again, when it conducted the 1976 Canadian championship to locate the biggest pumpkin or squash in Canada.

That was the contest that brought Dill his first real

recognition, but it was for the heaviest squash, not pumpkin.

His victory, with an entry of a 336-pound Show King squash he had developed, was over an exceptionally good grower from Roland, Manitoba, Edgar Van Wyck, and it brought an invitation from the Circleville, Ohio, Pumpkin Show to compete there.

That show is the biggest of its kind and attracts upwards of 100,000 visitors a day, over a four-day event.

Officials of the Circleville show were aware of Dill's weight of 336 pounds, set at the Atlantic Winter Fair in Halifax a week earlier. They told him that if he had his weight certified by two Nova Scotia Department of Agriculture officials, it would be accepted at the World Series of Pumpkin and Squash in Ohio.

Dill's entry had been cut from the vine for over a week and he knew that it would lose weight by dehydration on a long trip to Ohio, but he felt confident with the government-certified weight.

As he tells the story from there, "On my arrival, I soon realized that I had a good chance at winning the competition if I hadn't lost too much weight. The Ohio pumpkin show officials realized that I was in contention of winning the overall World's Largest Squash title and quickly pointed out that I would have to reweigh to have an official placing.

"In reply, I mentioned that I had followed their directions and request in presenting official documents, but officials of the show stated that their rule had changed, so therefore I had no choice but to reweigh my entry. As luck had it for the American side, I had lost 11 pounds during 10 days off the vine and lost the contest by four pounds.

"The four-pound defeat was hard to swallow as we returned to Nova Scotia, but somehow it spurred me on in the years to come, in search of the great pumpkin."

The 1977 and 1978 seasons were quiet times on the

Leonard Stellpflug of Rush, N.Y., holds the squash record of 807
pounds in international competition.

international scene as no competitions were held and no
records were set.

Dill sparked international competition between Canada
and the United States once again in 1979, when he set a new
giant pumpkin record of 438.5 pounds, at the United States
Cornell Pumpkin Show in Philadelphia. That victory broke
Warnock's previous international record set 76 years earlier
and was featured in *Ripley's Believe It or Not.*

Like any international competitor, Dill soon found out
that life on the road was not as glamorous as it might appear.

"After my first couple of seasons competing abroad, I
was starting to ask myself, 'What in the world was I thinking

about, travelling all the way from Nova Scotia to the states of Ohio and Pennsylvania with giant pumpkins?'

"It sure wasn't a profitable venture back then for making the 3,200-mile road trip in return for a ribbon at one show and a small cash award at the other."

Financial assistance from the Province of Nova Scotia was hard to come by but on his first trip, in 1976, Windsor Agricultural Society, Windsor Board of Trade and Bob Lindsay, local member of the provincial legislature, presented him with a cheque for $1,000. On two later occasions, the provincial government gave $500.

Transportation for the first trip was supplied by Dill's brother-in-law, the late Leon Curry, and the following years, Bob McDonald, a Halifax car dealer, and Stephens and Yeaton Limited of Windsor loaned a station wagon and a van

Norman Gallagher paid $10 in 1984 for enough seeds to grow a 612-pound pumpkin which won him $10,000, a trip for two to Hawaii, and a spot in the *Guinness Book of World Records*.

Dill is welcomed home with the Atlantic Giant which won him the triple crown in 1980. With him are, from left, wife Hilda and children Andrew, Diana, Danny and Maureen.

to transport pumpkins to U.S. competitions.

The 1980 season was another exciting year for Dill as he went back to Philadelphia and won his second international pumpkin growing championship with a 459-pound Atlantic Giant. The new record was publicized around the world by the Associated Press and Canadian Press news services and Canada's Maclean's magazine, which sent a photo agency from New York to Philadelphia to feature the achievement.

After the Philadelphia event, Dill, accompanied by his

Ray Waterman and Ayo Ogunbuyi grew the 780.5-pound WPC
champion for 1991 in Collins, N.Y.

cousin John Dill and his nephew Mike Trinacty, who brought
along his new bride Brenda, was soon on his way to Ohio. He
hoped to get his revenge at Circleville for being squashed by
the 1976 rule change.

The trip was worthwhile.

He tore through the American competition with a
vengeance, winning both the giant pumpkin and giant squash
competitions and setting new records in the process.

The (Halifax) *Chronicle-Herald* referred to his Canadian,
United States and international wins that year as the Triple
Crown of giant pumpkins.

But the 1981 season was to be an even more memorable
one as Dill won his third consecutive international
championship at Philadelphia with yet another record-

breaking specimen, weighing 493.5 pounds.

He then went on to win a second international weighoff, via the first telephone hookup between Half Moon Bay, California, and the Atlantic Winter Fair in Windsor. That new record was featured in the *Guinness Book of World Records* and thus became the pumpkin weight to beat in future competitions.

Because of those four forays to the United States, Dill is credited with starting the international competitions.

"I've never claimed that, but then I never argued the point either," he says. "Although perhaps it invented a new form of entertainment in popularizing giant pumpkins.

"Today, I guess we can only speculate as to what might have happened to the sport of growing giant pumpkins if I hadn't gone away."

Although the 1982 season failed to produce any new records, it did bring Dill his fourth consecutive international pumpkinship title with a 445-pounder.

That was the year which saw two New York growers, Ray Waterman and Harold Steff, compete at the Atlantic Winter Fair in Windsor. They brought a 319.5-pound specimen which placed third behind Dill's son Danny's second-place finisher in the international weighoff.

Dill recalls, "That's when I met Ray Waterman for the first time and could see his enthusiasm for giant pumpkins and where it could lead. After our friendly conversation, I quickly realized how serious Mr. Waterman was about the sport of giant pumpkins. Shortly after he returned home to Collins, New York, we conversed several times about the direction in which the giant pumpkin competition should go.

"Mr. Waterman felt that with what I had accomplished over the past four years the time was right to form a world competition involving other countries besides Canada and the United States. He was well aware that I was selling seed

Will Neily of Spa Springs, Annapolis County, N.S., grew Canada's
heaviest pumpkin in 1987. It weighed in at 587.6 pounds.
(Hants Journal)

to a company in the United Kingdom and felt that would be
a good place to start."

CHAPTER FOUR

WPC, IPA and GPC

AFTER HE ESTABLISHED his
friendship with Ray Waterman in the fall of 1982, Dill took
the proposition of a formal international competition to
David Coombes, secretary-manager of the Atlantic Winter
Fair, and Terry Pimsleur, co-ordinator of the Half Moon Bay
Pumpkin Show in California. They agreed a world weighoff
was a great idea.

During the winter and spring months that followed,
several conference calls took place among Dill, Coombes,
Waterman, Pimsleur and Ian Parsons of England, to sow the
seeds for what would grow into the World Pumpkin
Confederation.

Aim of the confederation was to establish a forum of
weighoff sites, with a membership of interested growers.
Creating a media event was a secondary consideration.

Waterman says the WPC was fashioned very much after
Dill's own thinking, character, abilities, and his interest in the
sport.

Rules would be kept simple, but strict.

Anyone in the world could enter, as long as they joined
the WPC by the date of the contest. Entries had to be grown
in one's own country, but could be weighed at any official
WPC site.

In addition to pumpkins and squash, categories also were established to include giant watermelon and any other fruit, vegetable or flower of competitive merit.

Specimens entered in competition would have to be healthy, undamaged and free of any foreign material. To guard against any wrongdoing on the latter point, judges were given authority to X-ray an entry.

Organizers had to compromise on a common day and hour for simultaneous weighing. October 10, 1983, was chosen as the day. That was Columbus Day in the United States and Canadians would be celebrating Thanksgiving. The date would follow the second annual Collins Pumpkin Festival, but would precede the 13th annual Half Moon Bay Festival.

The hour of 1 p.m. New York time seemed suitable, as it coincided with 2 p.m. in Nova Scotia, 6 p.m. in England and 11 a.m. in California.

Suitable hand-carved plaques were commissioned from John E. Donahue of Springville, New York.

That first year's competition was made even more interesting by an offer from the Waterman Farm of $1,500 for the first American-grown pumpkin to weigh 500 pounds or more. In England, Unwins Seeds Ltd. sweetened the pot for British growers by putting up a £10,000 prize for a pumpkin which would break Dill's world record weight of 493.5 pounds.

The first WPC weighoff was scheduled for the autumn of 1983 at sites at Windsor, Nova Scotia; Collins, New York; Half Moon Bay, California; and East Sussex, England. Weights from the four sites would be exchanged through an international telephone hookup.

As growers in Nova Scotia gathered for their weighoff, they weren't facing as high monetary stakes as had been posted at other sites, but they were under pressure to retain

In 1988, Lanny Harbord, centre, Port Wade, Annapolis County (627 pounds), Howard Dill, right, (616) and Danny Dill (575.5) took top three places in the WPC weighoff at Windsor Pumpkin Festival. (Spencer)

the world crown which Dill had held for four years.

Owen Woodman of Falmouth, near Windsor, kept Nova Scotia's winning streak going by winning the weighoff with a 481-pound pumpkin. Dill came up five pounds short of claiming a fifth consecutive international championship, but finished a strong second.

The 1984 season brought the most memorable and most exciting weighoff to date.

The World Pumpkin Confederation offered a grand prize of $10,000 to the U.S. grower who succeeded in breaking Dill's *Guinness Book of World Records* weight of 493.5 pounds.

Likewise, the Unwins Seed Company of Great Britain and *Garden News* offered a grand prize of £10,000 ($14,000 US) to the British grower entering a world record pumpkin at the WPC site in Birmingham, England, plus a pair of World Airways tickets to California.

As the 1984 weighoff unfolded on October 8, an unknown grower, Norman Gallagher from Chelan, Washington, set an almost unbelievable record of 612 pounds, thus breaking Dill's record.

For his efforts, Gallagher received a grand prize of $10,000; a trip for him and his wife Ruth to Hawaii; plus a feature in *Guinness Book of World Records*. All for the $10.00 cheque he sent to Dill before planting time that year "for the best Atlantic Giant seed possible."

"As the great baseball announcer Mel Allen would say, 'How about that!'," Dill remarks.

The WPC co-ordinators planned a meeting at Collins for the following February to discuss issues for the next weighoff, but actual conference time was limited as Dill and Coombes got caught in a blinding snowstorm in Ontario and Pimsleur became stranded in Buffalo.

When they all finally reached their destination, they had a good meeting and settled all outstanding issues except who would control the headquarters for the WPC. Both Coombes and Dill sensed tension mounting between Pimsleur and Waterman as to whose office was going to run the organization.

The controversy gradually spread to involve Nova Scotia's representatives and split their allegiance.

Dill favored Waterman's position and the direction he wanted to take promotion of the sport.

Coombes supported Pimsleur and they eventually decided to form the International Pumpkin Association, with primary weighoff sites at Half Moon Bay Pumpkin Festival in

Bob Gancarz of Wrightstown, N.J., set a new record of
671 pounds in 1986.

California and the Atlantic Winter Fair in Halifax, Nova
Scotia.

The official WPC site in Nova Scotia returned to Dill's
home town, where the Windsor Pumpkin Festival was
established to host the event.

The dual 1985 competitions saw another two
previously-unknown growers win titles in their organizations.
Scott Cully of Sharon, Connecticut, won the WPC weighoff
with a 515.5-pound specimen and Michael Hodgson of River

Philip, Nova Scotia, became the IPA's first champion with a 531-pounder.

It was the 1986 season that saw Bob Gancarz of New Jersey arrive on the giant pumpkin scene with his record-setting 671-pounder, topping the previous record set by Norman Gallagher in 1984 by 59 pounds. The IPA winner that year was Edgar Van Wyck of Roland, Manitoba, who grew a 548-pound pumpkin.

In 1987, it was Vermont grower Donald Fleming's turn to grow the year's biggest pumpkin as he produced one which weighed in at 604.5 pounds, at the WPC site at Topsfield Fair in Massachusetts. At the Atlantic Winter Fair, Arthur Vesey of York, Prince Edward Island, claimed the IPA trophy with his 408-pound entry.

Donald Fleming of Morrisville, Vt., receives a big cheque for winning the WPC championship at Topsfield, Mass., in 1987.

Lanny Harbord, of Port Wade, one of the more enthusiastic giant pumpkin growers, brought the WPC title back to Nova Scotia in 1988 with a 627-pound pumpkin and another Nova Scotian, Keith Chappell of Upper Granville, brought home the IPA title when his entry of 633 pounds was weighed at the Atlantic Winter Fair.

By now, stories of giant pumpkins were becoming commonplace, but apparently not everyone was reading them.

Bob Levy, a Chicago businessman, wanted to buy Dill's 616-pound pumpkin which had placed second that year in the WPC weighoff. He wanted to display it in the Windy City.

Dill dutifully built a strong shipping crate for transporting a specimen of its size, provided a bed of straw to protect it and trucked the package to Halifax International Airport.

On its arrival at O'Hare International Airport in Chicago, United States customs agents became suspicious and called in the drug squad to investigate. They didn't believe there could be a pumpkin that big inside the crate.

Wide-eyed inspectors eventually agreed to admit the oversize visitor, but the buyer later told Dill that it had taken longer to clear the giant pumpkin through customs than it did to have it flown halfway across the continent. The wait was worthwhile, though, as the pumpkin was a big hit and was viewed by thousands of people.

Despite its initial success and domination of pumpkin weighoffs, the World Pumpkin Confederation fell into disfavor with many of its top participants and supporters, including Dill, in 1993. Members were upset that Waterman was issuing few editions of what was supposed to be a quarterly newsletter; prize money was not being awarded in full, or not at all, because the WPC was canvassing for contributions for prizes, over and above its membership dues

Lloyd Smith presents Arthur Vesey, founder of Vesey's Seeds in
York, P.E.I., with an award as the oldest exhibitor at a Windsor
Pumpkin Festival. (Spencer)

and site fees; and the WPC never issued a financial
statement.

This dissatisfaction led to the development of a new
organization in 1993. The Great Pumpkin Commonwealth
was formed, and held weighoffs at Nut Tree, California;
Anamosa, Iowa; Topsfield, Massachusetts; and Windsor,
Nova Scotia. Additional sites were added, and in 1996
weighoffs were held at 18 locations.

The GPC quickly established itself as a major
contender in the pumpkin sweepstakes when its sites
claimed new world records in 1993 and 1994.

The Commonwealth cracked the 1,000-pound mark
in 1996, when Bill Greer, of Picton, Ontario, grew a giant that
weighed in at 1,006 pounds.

CHAPTER FIVE

BIGGER AND
BIGGER

JUST WHEN IT APPEARED that any further increase in giant pumpkin weights would be gradual, Gordon Thomson came out of his garden in the fall of 1989 at Hemmingford, Quebec, and drove to the weighoff site at Collins, New York. There, as Dill puts it, "he delivered the shot that was heard around the pumpkin world."

His Atlantic Giant weighed 755 pounds, and claimed the World Pumpkin Confederation record. Owen Woodman, of Falmouth, Nova Scotia, won his first International Pumpkin Association championship that year with a 533.5-pounder.

The world of vines and seeds was shocked again in 1990 when Ed Gancarz of New Jersey grew an 816.5-pound pumpkin, and set a new world record. Darren Woodworth, of Berwick, grew a 658-pound pumpkin in Nova Scotia to take the IPA crown that year.

Ray Waterman of Collins, New York, took his turn at claiming his organization's crown in 1991 with his entry of 780.5 pounds. At the IPA weighoff, Rod Harvey, of Newport, kept that trophy in Nova Scotia for yet another year, with his entry of 714 pounds.

Dill was happy that year to tip his cap to Waterman as a

driving force behind the WPC. "His efforts are to be commended, along with the others who have grown world champions over the years."

Joel Holland, Puyallup, Washington, set a new world record in 1992, with an 827-pound pumpkin weighed at the World Pumpkin Confederation site at Nut Tree, California. Veteran grower Owen Woodman, who had previously won

Gordon Thomson of Hemmingford, Que., delivered the shot heard round the pumpkin world in 1989, when he produced a 755-pound Atlantic Giant and increased the world record by 122 pounds.

Dill, left, poses with his WPC Lifetime Service and Achievement Award presented in 1991, when Lanny Harbord, centre, and Will Neily took top places in the Windsor Pumpkin Festival. (Kingsbury)

titles in both organizations, took top prize in the International Pumpkin Association with his entry of 587.5 pounds.

In 1993, a new grower and a new organization dominated the international pumpkin patch. Donald Black, of Winthrop, New York, trucked his giant pumpkin to Windsor, Nova Scotia, where the Dill's Atlantic Giant seeds began, to set a new world record of 884 pounds, in the first weighoff held by the Great Pumpkin Commonwealth. Norm Craven, Stouffville, Ontario, was the World Pumpkin Confederation's champion that year; and Joel Holland was back in the winner's circle with a 782-pounder, this time claiming victory in the International Pumpkin Association.

Although the most enthusiastic growers had by now begun to predict that the 1000-pound threshold would be crossed by the turn of the century, nobody was prepared to see Herman Bax of Lyn, Ontario, miss that target by just 10 pounds in 1994. He weighed in with a 990-pound world champion at a Great Pumpkin Commonwealth site at Ottawa.

That year, the International Pumpkin Association was a distant second, with a top weight of 799 pounds by Nathan Zehr, Lowville, New York; and the World Pumpkin Confederation trailed at 767 pounds, with the entry by Chris Lyons, of Scarborough, Ontario.

No world record was set in 1995, but Paula Zehr, of Lowville, New York, set a new United States record of 968 pounds, and dominated both the International Pumpkin Association and the Great Pumpkin Commonwealth. Norm Craven claimed his second WPC championship that year with his effort of 789 pounds.

Although enthusiasts had speculated that someone might break the 1,000-pound barrier by the turn of the century, few could have foreseen that being achieved as early as 1996, and certainly not by more than one grower.

But it happened. Nathan and Paula Zehr went to Clarence, New York, and weighed in with their entry of 1,061 pounds. Their prize was $50,000, offered by the World Pumpkin Confederation.

On the same day, just north of the border, Bill Greer, of Picton, Ontario, set a new Canadian and Great Pumpkin Commonwealth record of 1,006 pounds.

CHAPTER SIX

WEIGHOFF DAY

IT DAWNS LIKE MOST October mornings in Nova Scotia, cool and damp.

At 7 a.m., Howard Dill walks to the plot of prize pumpkins at the edge of his orchard, following the ritual he has observed every day for the past two months.

But this morning is different. Instead of a measuring tape to plot the growth progress of his "babies," he is carrying a large knife. His mission is to sever the stems from the vines which have been the pumpkins' umbilical cords, carrying nutrients and moisture for the giant natural factories for the past two months.

For most Canadians, it's Thanksgiving Day. For Howard Dill and giant-pumpkin enthusiasts around the world, it's Weighoff Day for the World Pumpkin Confederation.

Family and friends soon gather amid the jungle of vines for the ritual that will be repeated in gardens from Windsor to Washington.

The blade flashes in the early-morning sun as vines are cut away to make room to manoeuvre the giant gourds. One can feel the tension as each pumpkin is carefully rolled on its side to examine the shells for any sign of disease or rot.

A special tarpaulin, fitted with strong handles, is carefully slipped under each pumpkin and half a dozen pairs

Fans watch the weighoff at Windsor Pumpkin Festival. (Kingsbury)

of strong arms strain to lift the specimens from their birthplaces.

No limousine or even a special carriage awaits what might be the star of the day's news. Instead, it's a short and unceremonious ride in the back of a half-ton truck to the grounds of Kingsway Inn.

There an early-morning crowd has already gathered, many of them volunteers who have organized the Windsor Pumpkin Festival and who will spend the day supervising the local weighoff or operating booths and attractions to raise funds for local causes.

Other trucks and vans arrive, adding their orange and green giants to the display of color growing under the large canvas canopy. The crowd grows as the curious hesitantly

Entries await weighoff time at the WPC weighoff at
Collins, N.Y. (Addison)

walk among the entries, wanting to touch the giants of nature and inquiring as to which ones belong to whom, all the while secretly trying to predict the winners.

"Is that one Howard's?"

"Where are Will Neily's?"

"Has Lanny Harbord arrived yet?"

"Is Owen Woodman entering this year?"

At 11 a.m., the officials clear the area. They carefully inspect each entry to confirm that it is sound and eligible to be weighed.

After the scales are adjusted, six able men carry each of the entries forward.

For Howard Dill and his challengers, the moment of truth has arrived.

Cameras click and television crews jockey for the best positions as the crowd watches in anticipation, bursting into applause and cheers as favorite competitors retain their supremacy or a newcomer scores an upset.

The local weights are tallied and now the real suspense begins.

Spectators wonder aloud:

"Surely the Australians can't beat our weights."

"What kind of a growing season did they have in the States?"

Throughout the lunch hour, competitors congratulate each other and nervously answer questions from media and fair goers.

Around them, the carnival activities continue. Pumpkin pies and handcrafts are sold and local musicians belt out the current crop of top country tunes.

A local cow, appropriately dubbed Patty for the occasion, grazes over a section of lawn that has been ruled off to resemble a checkerboard. Around the enclosure, anxious players urge her to drop her first deposit on their squares so

Alicia Smith, right, was crowned Little Miss Pumpkin and Hollie Dawson was runner-up, at the 1985 Windsor Pumpkin Festival. (Kingsbury)

they can claim victory in the game of Pumpkin Patty Bingo.

By 2 p.m. (10 a.m. in California; 1 p.m. in Collins, New York; and 6 p.m. in E. Sussex, England), there's no need for an announcement that it's time for the international weighoff.

The telephone on the podium rings and Town Crier Lloyd Smith takes the call from Ray Waterman in Collins, New York, headquarters of the World Pumpkin Confederation. Waterman has others on the line from weighoff centres in other parts of Canada and the United States, as well as Britain.

Growers south of the equator, whose season is opposite, have already submitted their weights which have been kept secret.

Each spokesperson in turn reports the top three weights in each of pumpkin, squash and watermelon categories as the expectant crowd hangs on every weight heard over the loudspeakers.

There's a chuckle as they scoff at the meagre weights reported from one location. A sigh of relief greets the results from veteran contenders. Is this the year there will be a collective gasp as a new, unbelievable record is set?

No matter the outcome, there are congratulations to the local champions and to the new Pumpkin King. If Windsor hasn't taken all the prizes, wait 'til next year!

Only one is certain to go home a winner. Even if he has not personally produced the new world's champion, Howard Dill knows that it was one of his Atlantic Giant seeds that did.

CHAPTER SEVEN

HOBBY TO BUSINESS

LIKE ANY GOOD major league competitor, Howard Dill has parlayed his sporting achievements into a successful business.

With help from his family and worldwide interest in the sport of giant pumpkin growing, he has developed his passion into a thriving seed business.

But apart from a few significant sales, income has not come from his big pumpkins. Instead, it is generated from the seeds they and their offspring produce.

Dill's Atlantic Giant seeds are now marketed virtually all over the world, both through large international seed companies and through mail orders filled at the Dill family farm on College Road in Windsor, Nova Scotia.

It's not something that he planned or could even have foreseen, but as sometimes happens with small enterprises, this one has grown almost as fast as the giant fruit that are the centre of it all.

It all started after he won his first world pumpkin title in 1979. World interest, through printed and electronic media, suddenly centered on Howard Dill and his Atlantic

Giant pumpkins and requests for seeds started coming in.

His first major inquiry was from the Burgess Seed Company in the United States, which requested 400 pounds as an initial order. At more than 1,200 per pound, that translated to half a million seeds, many more than Dill was producing in his small farm plot.

It was then that he realized he had to expand, so he contracted with Hollar and Company in Colorado and Western Hybrids Seed Company of California to reproduce seed on two acres of land in each state.

Two other varieties, Big Mac and Big Moon, were producing pumpkins in the 200-pound range, which was fine for local contests, but not for world competition.

Noting the ever-increasing weights of the Atlantic Giant and the growing interest in the hobby, additional seed companies began placing orders and soon the reproduction acreage was increased to a total of 10 acres.

At about the same time, the large Unwins Seed Company in Great Britain contracted for exclusive rights to sell the Atlantic Giant for a few years. That agreement has since expired, but Unwins "will still bless you with a good order every year," Dill says.

It was then that the astute businessman realized he should have protection for his Atlantic Giant variety through the United States Department of Agriculture. The two-year wait for official recognition under the Plant Variety Protection Act caused many sleepless nights, but Dill now considers getting the certificate that was issued in 1986 "the greatest thing I ever did," as far as his business is concerned.

The certificate, signed by the United States Secretary of Agriculture, gives Dill the right to exclude others from selling the variety, offering it for sale, reproducing it, importing or exporting it, or using it to produce a hybrid or different variety.

Danny Dill fills mail orders received at the family farm in Windsor.
(Kingsbury)

Legislation is still pending to permit similar protection to be obtained in Canada.

The companies producing seed for Dill now have 10 acres each under cultivation. They produce and dry the seed, and then fill the major orders.

More than 2,000 pounds of Dill's Atlantic Giant seed are sold annually to several companies in Canada, the United States, Britain, Europe, Australia and Japan.

Another 15 pounds of seed from their own breeding plot enable the Dills to fill the 5,000 individual orders they receive at their Windsor home each year.

As might be expected, the home-based business has become a family affair.

Dill's wife of 34 years, the former Hilda Levy, attends to catalogue requests and his oldest daughter Maureen looks

Envelopes with some unusual and unique addresses have found their
way to the Dill home on College Road in Windsor. (Kingsbury)

after the typing for replies to letters and faxes.

Eldest son Danny records all the individual order
requests, carefully listing names and addresses for reference.
Dill's sister Margaret does most of the seed counter displays
that go out to nursery and garden seed centres and to gift
shops, and the two youngest children, Diana and Andrew,
help out in various ways when the pace really gets busy.

Dill's role is attending to all the mail orders, seed
company orders and exports of seed abroad, as well as paying
the bills.

The Atlantic Giant is being grown each year by an
estimated 10,000 serious pumpkin contest competitors and
perhaps millions of home gardeners.

The Dills have the advantage of never having to

Atlantic Giant seeds are sold in a variety of packets, printed in many languages, around the world.

Pumpkin awards, ornaments and memorabilia decorate the Dills'
home. (Kingsbury)

advertise their business. World media attention does it for
them.

Dill and his giant pumpkins have been the subject of
feature articles in about 40 magazines, and he has been
interviewed and featured in countless newspapers, newscasts
and radio and television programs.

Seeds sell for $3.50 for a packet of seven that could
produce 400-pounders. For something in the 500- to 700-
pound range, the price is $1.00 per seed. Those quantities
are not followed too closely, though. "I will throw in a few
extra, because I like to see them have good luck," Dill
confides.

CHAPTER EIGHT

FAME AND

FORTUNE

PROBABLY NOT SINCE Judge Thomas Chandler Haliburton put Windsor on the map with his tales of the fictional Yankee peddler Sam Slick, in his *Clockmaker* series, has this small Nova Scotian town received as much attention as it has since Howard Dill started growing world-champion pumpkins.

And there are few Canadians of any background or profession who have received so much international media exposure or are as well known outside their own country.

Dill's pumpkin-growing exploits have been the subject of countless feature articles in newspapers and magazines, and interviews have been carried by national and international broadcast networks.

He was listed in the *Guinness World Book of Records* in 1981 as grower of the world's heaviest pumpkin.

Ripley's Believe It or Not featured his pumpkins on three different occasions in its syndicated newspaper cartoon feature. In 1980, it was a drawing of Dill's wife Hilda curled up in the hollowed-out shell of a 438.5-pound pumpkin; the following year Dill himself showed his 459-pounder; and in 1983, Dill was back in the feature with the world's largest jack-o'-lantern, which he had carved from a 445-pound pumpkin.

His exploits have brought such recognition to Windsor that it has been able to lay claim to the title of *Pumpkin Capital of the World.*

Dill has been the subject of textbooks and documentaries and tourists by the busload find their way up the narrow driveway to his College Road farm for a personal tour of his pumpkin patch, conducted by the Pumpkin King himself.

With his unassuming manner, he must be the envy of every publicist, because he rarely seeks any attention. It just

Hilda Dill shows that nursery rhyme character Peter Peter really could have put his wife in a pumpkin shell and "kept her very well." This photo was used as the basis for a drawing in *Ripley's Believe It or Not* syndicated newspaper feature. (Davidson)

Dill dressed in his Sunday best to talk about his pumpkin exploits on Canada AM. (Doucette)

seems to be drawn to him as bees to a flower on one of his pumpkin vines.

As many as 5,000 letters are delivered to the Dill mailbox every year, most containing orders for seeds and many with addresses as incomplete as: "Dill," Windsor; Pumpkin Grower Extraordinaire; or just a colored picture of a giant pumpkin with his name on it.

Perhaps the most unusual piece of mail came from a lawyer acquaintance in Halifax, who also is a friend of former Nova Scotia premier John Buchanan.

It was in 1981, when Dill was just becoming widely known as the world pumpkin champion and Buchanan was in office for only a few years.

In a mischievous experiment, the lawyer addressed an envelope by pasting a newspaper picture of Dill on it and adding the words, "Windsor, N.S." He addressed another envelope in a similar manner to the premier.

Within a matter of days, Dill had his letter. There's no word whether the other piece of mail ever reached its destination.

Phone calls can come any time of the day or night, from anywhere in the world, interrupting farm chores or sleep.

Whatever the time, or whoever the caller, there's always time to offer growing advice or to compare notes on how each other's best prospects are developing as weighoff time approaches.

It's not unusual for a film crew to drop in unannounced and expect Dill to spend several hours working with them and answering questions, nor for the famous to seek out someone who has reached the top in a different calling.

Dill delights in telling the story of the day the tall, athletic stranger dropped in to see his pumpkins. As they carefully picked their steps through the tangle of vines feeding the current crop of pumpkins, it was the Super Bowl ring that gave the first hint of the visitor's identity. The Miami Dolphins jacket confirmed that football wasn't the only sport that interested quarterback Earl Morrall. He later sent an autographed picture and his good wishes.

In 1982, just a few years after Dill started achieving fame, Canada's vice-consul in San Francisco wrote to a Nova Scotia member of parliament. He reported that Dill's success in trouncing American contenders at a California weighoff had generated "the most press attention Canada has had on the Peninsula in quite a while and the most Nova Scotia has had in my time here."

When a Toronto communications agency was preparing an information package for Canada's Metric Commission to

This 1979 picture shows Dill with some of his first major awards for winning Canadian and international championships. The seeds on the plaque are out of that year's international winner. (Spencer)

educate Canadians about metric measurements, it used a picture of Dill and two of his children with the world's largest pumpkin of the time. The accompanying description, circulated in both English and French, gave the pumpkin's dimensions in metric measurements.

Dill packed up one of his Atlantic Giants and an assortment of smaller pumpkins to send to Canada's warships patrolling the Persian Gulf in 1990.

International magazines have featured Dill and his big pumpkins — and often neighborhood children as well — in cover stories, and in 1991 he was listed in a book of Canada's top achievers.

Fans and admirers across the country have been moved to write poems about his exploits as their way of paying tribute.

With a name like his and being the leading contender in such an unusual sport, it was inevitable that Howard Dill would be the butt of creative headline writers.

If he has a winner, it's bound to be referred to as a "dilly," which perhaps has "squashed" the competition. If he falls short of the championship, or there's a disaster in his pumpkin patch, Dill can expect to read that he's in a "pickle." How is he ranked among pumpkin growers? Why, "top-seeded," of course.

Dill's prize pumpkins have been sought after and have been exhibited in commercial displays from Texas to Alberta and along the way they have been used to help others.

The Dartmouth (Nova Scotia) Lions Club has set world records for the most pies baked from a single pumpkin (442) and sold them at auction to raise funds for Oakwood Terrace seniors residence.

One of his pumpkins was so sought after that thieves stole it from a fair in Kleinburg, Ontario, and held it for ransom at $1 a pound. The plot was foiled, though, when Dill promptly contributed another 400-pounder and Air Canada provided free air freight to transport the replacement to Toronto.

Chef Brenton Hubley pours filling into some of the 442 pies which set a record for the most pies made from a single pumpkin. The pies were sold by Dartmouth Lions Club to raise funds for Oakwood Terrace senior citizens home. (Danch)

Dill has sold several of his giants to supermarkets, businesses and farm markets, not only in Nova Scotia, but also in Miami, Houston, Chicago and Edmonton.

Perhaps the most unusual request, though, came from the Canadian Armed Forces during the fall of 1990, when three of Canada's warships were preparing for service in the Persian Gulf.

Touted at the time as a "new secret weapon," because of the menacing grin it was to have when made into a giant jack-o'-lantern, the pumpkin was designed to be a morale booster for Canada's service men and women half a world away from home.

Dill sent along enough smaller pumpkins so that each ship would have a reminder of happier times being celebrated as families waited for their loved ones to return.

For his contribution to the war effort, which included the $500 worth of seeds in the big pumpkin, Dill received a signed certificate from Canada's minister and associate minister of defence and the chief of the defence staff.

That award, along with numerous other items of memorabilia, decorate the Dill farmhouse. There are trophies, ribbons, plaques and calendars. Even the new hearth he built a few years ago around the wood stove in the kitchen is rounded to mimic the shape of a pumpkin.

A plaque bearing the coat-of-arms of the town of Windsor recognizes his achievements in bringing home the world championship for pumpkin growing.

The World Pumpkin Confederation paid him special honor at the 1991 weighoff.

With Ray Waterman reading a citation by telephone from Collins, New York, and Lloyd Smith making the physical presentation at the Windsor Pumpkin Festival, Dill was given a WPC Lifetime Service and Achievement Award and inducted as the first member of the Giant Pumpkin Hall

Barbara Frum (Willer)

of Fame.

His scrapbooks and boxes of files include recipes for every manner of preparing pumpkin and squash for eating; folklore tales; pictures and souvenirs from pumpkin shows and championship weighoffs in Canada and the United States; and records of pumpkin-growing competitions.

The Tourism Industry Association of Nova Scotia

recognized Dill's efforts in promoting his native province when it awarded him its Ambassador Award of Excellence in 1995. The award recognizes an individual or organization which has personally excelled in efforts to develop tourism on a provincial or national basis, and whose activities have made a major impact on tourism and culture in the province.

Although Dill's name has gone around the world and back again, he's never forgotten the individuals in the media, both at the national and local levels, who first gave him their attention.

Topping his list is the late Barbara Frum, host of the CBC radio program *As It Happens* and later *The Journal* on CBC television, who was responsible for his first national exposure. Over the years, Frum interviewed him on four different occasions.

It was Gordon Murray, then a reporter for *The Chronicle-Herald*, who was responsible for the first front-page feature on the provincial level, and CBC-TV was first on the scene with television cameras.

Lloyd Smith, of Windsor radio station CFAB, was the first Annapolis Valley reporter to conduct an interview, and the local weekly, *The Hants Journal*, highlighted many early championship victories, as did Harold Woodman, then editor of the (Kentville) *Advertiser*.

Other notable news media which helped put the sport of giant pumpkins on the map were CTV, through *Canada AM*, *Live It Up* and *W5*, and CBC Radio's *Information Morning*.

Dill also has been featured on such television programs as CBC's *Marketplace, Business World* and *Country Canada*, *Ripley's Believe It or Not, Inside Edition and Reading Rainbow*.

He was also seen in a cameo appearance in a movie, *Buried on Sunday*, cowering beside one of his giant pumpkins as a Russian missile goes overhead in an attack on Nova Scotia.

CHAPTER NINE

WHAT IS A PUMPKIN?

J UST WHAT IS a pumpkin?
Is it a gourd? A fruit? A vegetable?

The simple answer is that it is all three.

Technically speaking, it is one of the long-keeping varieties of the Cucurbitaceae family, more commonly known as gourds. The pumpkin is the fruit of the Cucurbita Pepo plant, a cousin of Cucurbita maxima, which most of us call squash.

The real confusion comes from the fact that some structures of plants, which are certainly fruits in a technical sense, are popularly called vegetables.

According to *Encyclopedia Americana*, the term vegetable, which is not a technical one, could well be restricted to any edible portion of a plant, usually not intimately associated with the flower in development. However, usage of these terms is so well established that technical distinctions are not likely.

Pumpkins are believed to have originated in South America, probably Peru and Chile. They gradually spread north and were in common use among the Indians at the time of the early colonization of North America.

Pilgrims who were introduced to pumpkins enjoyed a diet that was at times bountiful but always limited in variety. That prompted a member of the Plymouth colony of 1623 to compose the following ditty:

> Instead of pottage and puddings and custards and pies;
> Our pumpkins and parsnips are common supplies;
> We have pumpkin at morning and pumpkin at noon;
> If it was not for pumpkin we should be undoon.

Today, pumpkins are grown throughout the United States, Canada and many other countries.

The word pumpkin derives from an old French word pompion, which itself comes from the Latin word pepo, that signified among the ancients a melon. The old English writer Elyot writes of "a kind of melones called pompones."

H. K. Meyer writes in *Organic Gardening* that "the word pompion was more used before 1600 than the present form pumpkin. Amusingly enough, the first reference to pumpkin is 'our pumpkin blasted brains,' which somewhat reminds us of pumpkin-heads."

From a seed production point of view, squash and pumpkin are grown and handled in much the same way.

Unfortunately, the terms squash and pumpkin have been applied rather loosely to various varieties without regard to the species of Cucurbita to which they belong. There has thus developed a classification based more on its vegetable usage than on its botanical or even its horticultural characteristics.

Two of America's greatest horticulturists, Erwin and Bailey, often exchanged views and detailed studies to classify all the common varieties into three botanical species, namely: c. Pepo, c. Moschata and c. Maxima.

In view of the many studies and varied publications

Dill not only grows the big pumpkins, but also turns his hand at carving the world's largest jack-o'-lantern. (Spencer)

dealing with this problem of the classification of squash and pumpkin, both botanically and as a vegetable, it was proposed in the discussion that the terms pumpkin and squash both be used in the sense that they are commonly referred to in most seed catalogues. The idea, however, was not well accepted by their customers and today most seed catalogues ignore a strict botanical classification.

The U.S. National Garden Bureau, which is celebrating 1992 as the Year of the Pumpkin, gets right to the point with

Neighborhood children in Hallowe'en costume walk through the Dill pumpkin patch. (Spencer)

Hilda Dill serves an assortment of pumpkin goodies to a group of
visiting agriculture dignitaries. (Spencer)

this simple explanation:

"If it looks like a pumpkin, tastes like a pumpkin and
carves like a pumpkin — it is a pumpkin."

For the seed grower and breeder, an accurate
knowledge of what species and variety the fruit belongs to is
important because of the problems of either preventing
cross-pollination by isolation or actually attempting it in
some breeding programs.

The classification of some varieties of pumpkins and
squash is frequently confusing as they may carry different
designations with different growers, or in different parts of
the country.

Horticultural references mention this confusion and the
fact that in some districts these words are used

indiscriminately.

From a technical standpoint, the giant pumpkin is probably best termed squash, but many gardeners will likely refer to it as pumpkin.

Despite all its attractive and legendary characteristics, the pumpkin is not just a showy autumn entertainer, good for harvest displays and Hallowe'en jack-o'-lanterns. It is a nutritious item of food.

Early Pilgrims concocted the first version of pumpkin pies by slicing off the top, scraping out the cavity and then filling it with apples, sugar, spices and milk. The top was replaced and the stuffed fruit was baked whole.

In their inventive ways, they used pumpkins for almost anything from stews and soups to beer and pumpkin chips.

Pumpkins and their squash cousins also were recommended for health and beauty aids.

Seeds pounded with meal removed freckles; seeds were a good worm expellant; whole squash (in quantity) was recommended for snakebite; pulverized seeds in water were taken for bladder trouble; and tea of ground pumpkin stems treated "female ills."

Pains of childbirth, toothache and chilblains were said to abate if one chewed on a squash, and Jamestown colonists used boiled squash mashed into paste as a poultice for sore eyes.

For human consumption today, the pumpkin's chief use is in pies, providing a rich source of carbohydrates, calcium and iron. Large fruited varieties have been used as feed for stock, but are now grown primarily for competition.

In some areas, especially Europe, oil is recovered from its seeds. A nut-like delicacy is made by roasting and salting kernels of pumpkin seed.

Like all gourds, Pepos grow on large-leaved, rapidly-developing, tendril-supported vines, but are distinguished by

Donald Black of Winthrop, was the first grower to break the 600-pound barrier in New York, when he grew this 625-pounder in 1989. Black is well known as the "eyes and ears" of the WPC.

A giant pumpkin dominates a harvest display at the Dill farm.
(Spencer)

their tough outer wall. Flowers are of two types: the male
(staminate) flowers, producing pollen; and the female
(pistillate) flowers, forming the fruit. In most forms, both
types of flowers are found on the same vine.

CHAPTER TEN

GROWING THE
BIG ONES

For EVERY SUCCESSFUL grower of giant pumpkins there is bound to be some secret or at least variation of technique, but for the most part, it's just good standard growing practices that bring success.

It is sometimes claimed that unusual fruit size of pumpkin and squash can be obtained by various techniques of milk feeding, but few qualified and experienced growers endorse such procedures. They would generally agree that careful attention to regular cultural practices has greater merit.

For example, the late William Warnock of Goderich, Ontario, presented his own set of growing directions back in 1905 on how he grew his world champion specimens.

> My land is made in good condition. Being heavily manured every year, it is of gravelly formation with about 16 inches of clay loam on top.
> A 300-pound squash or pumpkin can be grown on any part of it by the following method

cultivation: For each hill I intend to plant, about the first of April I take two good wheelbarrow loads of hen manure and mix with four barrows of good soil taken from some other part of the lot. This is mixed a second time the middle of April.

The first week of May, I make the hills and plant, dig out a space seven feet in diameter and 14 inches deep; fill in my compost mixing and with it some of the best earth which was thrown out and when finished, the hills will be about 10 feet in diameter and six inches higher in the centre than the surrounding level. Then plant the seed.

Hills want to be about 20 feet apart; work the ground well until the plants commence to run. When about three feet long, I mulch the ground all over for 20 feet in diameter around each hill with horse manure, three inches deep, and stake the vines down with sticks to keep the wind from rolling them about, so that they may root at every joint. It is of great advantage to keep the vine from fruiting as long as possible, by pruning all fruit bloom off until about the last week in July; this will give time enough to mature a 300-pound pumpkin or squash by the first of October, for there must be a big vine to produce a big pumpkin or squash.

I practice fertilizing a few of the first blooms that come, when I think the vine is strong enough to grow a good specimen, by cutting off some of the fresh male bloom, trim the corolla or flower leaf off and rub the stamen in around the fresh fruit bloom.

This is necessary when fruit bloom opens on a morning that is unfavorable for bees to do their work and it assures the setting of the specimens just where you want them. It also gives extra vigor

Keith Chappell's 633-pound IPA champion exhibited at the Atlantic Winter Fair in Halifax in 1988. (Slaunwhite)

to the growth of fruit to be well pollinated.

When the first perfect specimens have set well, say four or five inches in diameter, cut all other fruit and blossoms off and nip the ends off vines and all bloom that shows, twice a week, so that the vine is not exhausted with the great quantity of false blooms that would naturally come.

Now while the great growth of the pumpkin or squash is going on, I use liquid manure twice a week along the three or four of the principal vines of each hill, often six pails to a hill if it is in a dry time. Great care must be taken to give plenty of water.

For instance, in 1893, when I grew the great specimen that was the largest on exhibition at the World's Fair, it was a dry time with us at Goderich, and having the advantage of the town water service, I sprayed each hill twice a week through August and the first two weeks in September, drenching the ground each time.

P.S. — I expect all have heard of feeding pumpkin and squash by injecting milk or other stuff. This is a ridiculous, silly humbug. I have practiced several methods along this line when I was younger, but it only makes me ashamed to confess it, and I am now quite satisfied the only thing that will increase the size of the fruit comes out of the vine, and the vines must get support from the natural roots.

Howard Dill does not vary much from this age-old advice.

His Atlantic Giant is an enormously large pumpkin and is often seeded in a controlled environment. For areas where there is a danger of frost in late April or early May, he suggests starting seeds indoors about two weeks before

Dill builds plastic shelters to protect his young pumpkin plants from spring frosts. (Kingsbury)

planting. Fill four-inch peat pots with grow mix and sow one seed in each. Keep the pots watered.

When seedlings have four or five leaves, set them outdoors, one plant to a hill, which should be several yards square and about 20 feet apart. For their first few weeks, plants should be protected with plastic-covered cold frames.

Almost all vine crops such as pumpkins produce separate male and female flowers on each plant. Often the first few flowers to appear will be male and gardeners sometimes worry unnecessarily about this when they observe that no fruit is setting.

In a short time (approximately 10 days), however, female flowers (pistillate) will develop and fruit will begin to form under the flower. Female flowers can be distinguished from male by the tiny fruit buds which are seen at the base of

Disappointment shows on Dill's face as he weighs his top contender which fell victim to rot in 1990. (Kingsbury)

the petals. Male flowers (staminate) have only male parts and produce pollen.

The most effective time for pollination is between 8 and 10 a.m. and the ideal temperature is around 21 C (70 F).

In order to self-pollinate, try this simple method:

Pick off a newly-opened male flower and trim off the corolla flower leaf. Rub the pollen-laden stamen (a spur in the centre of the flower) around the inside of a newly-opened female flower. The female flower should receive several hundred pollen grains.

If pollination is left for bees, pistillate flowers should be visited by bees at least 10 to 12 times for satisfactory fruit set. The more pollen transferred, the more seed produced and the bigger the fruit.

As the plants grow, they become pumpkin-producing factories, with each leaf, stem and hair root receiving sunlight, absorbing water and blending nutrients to send through the main stem to the pumpkin.

Dill advises carefully pulling out roots of the vine near the pumpkin and training them out of the way. This avoids the possibility of the fruit pulling out the vine from the stem or crushing it as it grows to giant proportions.

The pumpkin's life cycle can be divided almost exactly in two, with the first 60 days or so taken up in seed germination, transplanting, development of the plant system and vine, and flowering.

During the second 60 days, the fruit develops and grows.

Dill points out that with only about a 60-day growth period, a 600-pound pumpkin must grow at an average of 10 pounds per day, which means that at its peak growth period it is adding 15 pounds or more each day.

Such growth rates can bring their own hazards, as Dill knows only too well. He has had the experience of being shocked during a morning inspection by finding one of his giants has literally exploded.

He reasons that on very hot days, pumpkins heat up inside and begin to cook. The flesh deteriorates and heat increases until the innards burst out.

In less dramatic instances, the walls can break down because they are not strong enough to support the tremendous weight being produced.

While he takes regular measurements of all his giant pumpkins, Dill says that is not an accurate method of forecasting weight.

"Thickness of the walls is the deciding factor. On giant specimens, walls can range from four to six inches thick."

The oblong shape of the immature fruit of Dill's Atlantic Giant is first noticeable at its earliest stage of development and when its pumpkin factories get into full production, vines can grow up to 10 inches per day and pumpkins can increase their weight by 15 to 20 pounds daily.

The general shape of the mature fruit, which is a yellow to orange color, will vary, depending on culture and rate of growth. Flattening will often occur because the structure of the rapidly growing fruit is not sufficient to the weight.

Growing for serious competition takes dedication and a competitive spirit. The Pumpkin King spends about two hours a day tending his show plot, which generally has about 14 plants and fills half an acre behind his house.

Care should be taken to protect the plants from wind and frost; cover them during heavy rains; and provide shade for the hottest days of summer. Plants should be sprayed or dusted to control insects.

The most common insect pest for eastern Canadian pumpkin and squash is the striped cucumber beetle. These pests feed on leaves, flowers and fruit of all vine crops and transmit diseases such as Bacterial Wilt and Mosaic Virus.

Daily measurements are taken of pumpkins to chart their growth after they pass the halfway mark of their development. (Kingsbury)

The beetle is yellow with three black stripes on its back. To help prevent attacks by adult beetles on the tender young plants, use an insecticide such as Malathion, Methoxychlor, Rotenone or Carbaryl (sold as Sevin). Dill prefers Rotenone for dusting young pumpkin plants.

The Vine Borer (Melittia Cucurbitae) can be very destructive and is found in several states of the United States. The first symptoms of feeding are wilting of the vine or a portion of it. The stem will be hollowed out, filled with a slimy froth from borer feeding. Occasionally, froth can be seen at the base of the plant, evidence of borer penetration. Affected vines normally rot and die.

The caterpillar is up to one inch (2.5 centimetres) long and white with a brown head. The insect overwinters in the soil as a larva or pupa. When the vines begin to run, the pupa surfaces and splits to release the small, black, wasp-like moth. The moth lays eggs on the basal portion of the stem and in one to two weeks, borers emerge and penetrate the stem. Control is difficult, but sprays (Methoxychlor, Carbaryl) are recommended and can be applied during egg laying and hatching.

Squash Bugs (Anasatristis) are distributed throughout all production areas. The adult, brownish black, flat-backed, 5/8 inches (15 millimetres) long, lays its eggs on the underside of leaves, usually in rows at a right angle. The eggs hatch, giving rise to bright-colored nymphs which, together with adults, feed on plant sap. The insect can kill small plants completely and cause leaves of large vines to wilt and die. Control recommendations are the same as for borers.

Other common insects are aphids, black rot, pickle worms, leafhoppers and spider mites.

CHAPTER ELEVEN

EVERYBODY'S GROWING THEM

So WHO'S GROWING all those giant pumpkins now?

With millions of Atlantic Giant seeds being sown around the world every year, it's obvious that more than farmers or even avid gardeners are getting into the sport.

Howard Dill's experience indicates that people from all walks of life, from the age of four to 90, are planting pumpkin seeds.

Many are not just growing the giants for their own enjoyment, but are participating in competitions in their local areas or within corporate or professional groups.

Three international organizations now are holding annual fall weighoffs, with entries from as many as 30 countries.

Participants cover the whole age spectrum, from children entering their first specimens to octogenarians continuing to pursue the hobby that brings both challenge and satisfaction, along with camaradarie of fellow growers across town and around the world.

For years, avid growers have kept in touch by letters and phone calls, but now the Internet has become involved. Grower Dan Gardner of Appleton, Wisconsin, has set up the "Unofficial Giant Pumpkin Homepage," at http://www. athena.athenet.net/~dang/pumpkins.html. His site includes information on international weighoffs; world records; and growing information. He has also set up a mail list server, an automatic electronic mailing service, through which growers can exchange information through cyberspace.

Frank Bray, of Lower Sackville, Nova Scotia, has also established an Internet site, at http://www.ips.ca/ibp/ neat_things/dills_pumpkins/. This Howard Dill's Giant

Giant pumpkin growing is a sport which knows no age boundaries. Octogenarian Jack Dill (Howard's cousin) receives an award as oldest exhibitor at Windsor Pumpkin Festival from announcer Lloyd Smith. (Spencer)

Pumpkins site also has information, and a complete ordering system for everything from seeds to carrying tarpaulins and pumpkin publications.

Actors Eddie Albert and the late Raymond Burr, best known respectively for their television series *Green Acres* and *Ironside*, were hooked on the sport of giant pumpkin growing.

Albert grew one over 400 pounds and Burr would have traded an Oscar for a 400-pounder.

Groups of police officers and firefighters, from New York to Vancouver, along with Wall Street executives, have organized growing contests among themselves.

Large corporations have sponsored competitions to spark interest within their sales staffs and among their top executives.

Probably the most unusual weighoff was held in San Francisco in 1990. A group of people near that California city decided they wanted to do something positive to mark the first anniversary of the 1989 earthquake which had devastated their area. They organized a pumpkin-growing contest, and held their weighoff at the precise moment that the earthquake had struck a year earlier.

Several years ago, Dill received a letter from a bank manager in Mobile, Alabama, saying he had seen a magazine article about Dill and his giant pumpkins.

The manager acknowledged that he was not known for having a green thumb, and was often reminded of this by his wife. For once in his life, he wrote, he wanted to surprise his wife — and maybe even himself — by growing something.

Dill filled his order for seeds and a few weeks later received payment in the form of silver dollars. Nothing more was heard until the fall, when a large envelope arrived from Alabama. Inside was a front page of the Sunday edition of the *Mobile Daily News*, carrying a color picture of the bank manager proudly showing his 335-pound pumpkin.

Four former world champion pumpkin growers gathered at Windsor, N.S., in 1993 to tip their hats to that year's record setter. Donald Black, of Winthrop N.Y., whose pumpkin weighed 884 pounds. From left are Howard Dill ('79, '80, '81, '82), Windsor, N.S.; Owen Woodman ('83), Falmouth, N.S.; Black; Norm Gallagher ('84), Chelan, Wash.; and Gordon Thomson ('89), Hemmingford, Que.

CHAPTER TWELVE

WHERE WILL

IT END?

Afterthe long, slow, lonely
process of developing his seed variety and gradually edging
his weights up to 100 pounds . . . 200 pounds . . . 300 pounds,
it's difficult even for Howard Dill to comprehend the
changes that have occurred since he made his first trip to the
United States in 1976, and stirred interest in international
pumpkin growing competition.

In those two decades, his Dill's Atlantic Giant variety
has become the sole producer of world champion pumpkins,
and is now sold and grown around the world.

He has personally won four consecutive world
championships, along with two international squash titles,
and he continues to be a strong contender. He has missed out
on regaining his world pumpkin title by only a few pounds.

Whether or not he's in the winner's circle himself on
weighoff day, Dill justly shares in the glory of every
champion, because they are all using his seeds.

Attention and honors have come from many quarters,
but none surpasses the recognition extended to him in 1991.
That's when he was awarded a Lifetime Service and

Achievement Award by the World Pumpkin Confederation, and inducted as the first member of the Giant Pumpkin Hall of Fame.

He was one of the founders of the WPC, and then became one of the charter growers and leaders of the Great Pumpkin Commonwealth. His son Danny, an active partner in the family seed business, serves as co-ordinator for the Windsor GPC weighoff site.

Once the 500-pound barrier was broken with a flourish in 1984, other weight targets were surpassed almost as fast as they were set. With the current world record standing at 1,061 pounds, serious growers eagerly look forward to each new weighoff, wondering when, and at what level, the ultimate record will be set.

Joel Holland of Puyallup, WA shown with his 1992 world record pumpkin that weighed 827 pounds.

Dill shows one of the seeds from this 445-pound pumpkin to son
Andrew as he carves a giant jack-o'-lantern. (Kingsbury)

Among those is Howard Dill, who has done more than
anyone else to promote the sport of giant pumpkin growing,
and for years has been the acknowledged world pumpkin
king.

As he looks back on the triumphs and attention that
have come his way, he turns to the people who have become
part of his life: the Watermans, Thomsons, Wibergs,
Gallaghers, Gancarzes, Stellpflugs and Rigolosos.

"Perhaps the nicest thing to come out of growing giant
pumpkins is the friendship that I have experienced among
growers," he says.

"I am doubtful if it wasn't for those early years
competing abroad that I would have ever gotten to meet or
know the Blacks, Glasiers, Hackneys, Grants, Flemings,
Nelsons, Cilibertos, Nesbitts, Chaponis, Wrights, Hurleys,

MacDonalds, Keyzers, Norlins, Mitchells."

The list goes on as he remembers "the Hollands, Rhodenizers, Casellos, Mangiones, Van Wycks, Cullys, Barbers, Schoenfelders, Winklers, Spinneys, Sorans, Browns, McGowans, Yandohs, Rizzos, and many more who have made giant pumpkin growing what it is today."

But enough of the past. New challenges lie ahead.

Ever looking to new goals, Dill says that while the 1996 growing season will go down in history for producing the first two 1,000-pound Dill's Atlantic Giant pumpkins, "the question now is, will we exceed the 1,500-pound pumpkin by the year 2000."

Paula Zehr, of Lowville, N.Y., grew the largest pumpkin in 1995. It weighed 968 pounds, and captured top honors in both the International Pumpkin Association and the Great Pumpkin Commonwealth. (Eaton)

96

RECORD

HOLDERS

Paula and Nathan Zehr, of Lowville, N.Y., set a new world pumpkin record in 1996, with a monster pumpkin that weighed 1,061 pounds. (Buffalo News)

WORLD CHAMPION PUMPKIN GROWERS

YEAR	GROWER	PLACE	WEIGHT
1979	Howard Dill	Windsor, NS	438.5
*1980	Howard Dill	Windsor, NS	459.0
*1981	Howard Dill	Windsor, NS	493.5
1982	Howard Dill	Windsor, NS	445.0
1983	Owen Woodman	Falmouth, NS	481.0
*1984	Norman Gallagher	Chelan, WA	612.0
1985	Michael Hodgson	River Philip, NS	531.0
*1986	Bob Gancarz	Wrightstown, NJ	671.0
1987	Don Fleming	Morrisville, VT	604.5
1988	Keith Chappell	Upper Granville. NS	633.0
*1989	Gordon Thomson	Hemmingford, QU	755.0
*1990	Ed Gancarz	Wrightstown, NJ	816.5
1991	Ray Waterman & Ayo Ogunbuyi	Collins, NY	780.5
*1992	Joel Holland	Puyallup, WA	827.0
*1993	Donald Black	Winthrop, NY	884.0
*1994	Herman Bax	Brockville, ON	990.0
1995	Paula Zehr	Lowville, NY	968.0
*1996	Nathan & Paula Zehr	Lowville, NY	1,061.0

*World Record

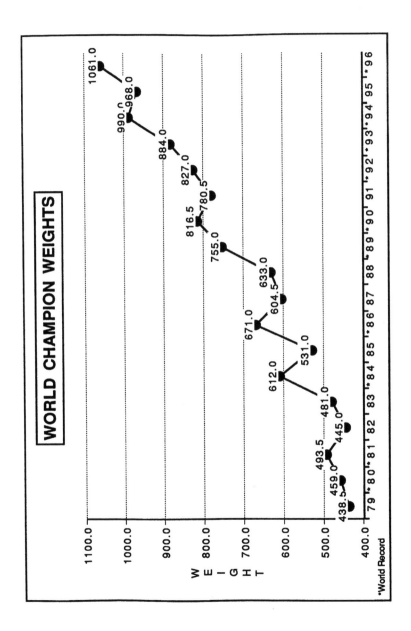

WORLD CHAMPION WEIGHTS

WORLD PUMPKIN CONFEDERATION

YEAR	GROWER	WEIGHT
1983	Owen Woodman, NS	481.0
*1984	Norman Gallagher, WA	612.0
1985	Scott Cully, CT	515.5
*1986	Bob Gancarz, NJ	671.0
1987	Don Fleming, VT	604.5
1988	Lanny Harbord, NS	627.0
*1989	Gordon Thomson, QU	755.0
*1990	Ed Gancarz, NJ	816.0
1991	Ray Waterman & Ayo Ogunbuyi, NY	780.5
*1992	Joel Holland, WA	827.0
1993	Norm Craven, ON	836.0
1994	Chris Lyons, ON	767.0
1995	Norm Craven, ON	789.0
*1996	Nathan and Paula Zehr, NY	1061.0

INTERNATIONAL PUMPKIN ASSOCIATION

1985	Michael Hodgson, NS	531.0
1986	Edgar Van Wyck, MAN	548.0
1987	Arthur Vesey, PEI	408.0
1988	Keith Chappell, NS	633.0
1989	Owen Woodman, NS	533.5
1990	Darren Woodworth, NS	658.0
1991	Rod Harvey, NS	714.0
1992	Owen Woodman, NS	587.5
1993	Joel Holland, WA	782.0
1994	Nathan Zehr, NY	799.0
1995	Paula Zehr, NY	968.0
1996	Takao Hoshigima, Japan	756.1

GREAT PUMPKIN COMMONWEALTH

*1993	Donald Black, NY	884.0
*1994	Herman Bax, ON	990.0
1995	Paula Zehr, NY	963.0
*1996	Bill Greer, ON	1006.0

*World Record

Herman Bax, of Brockville, Ontario, Canada, proudly embraces his 990-pound pumpkin. The world's largest vegetable was grown in 1994. (Jeff Bassett, Ottawa Sun)

CANADA'S LARGEST PUMPKINS

YEAR	GROWER	WEIGHT
1976	Howard Dill, Windsor, N. S .	336.0
1977	Howard Dill, Windsor, N . S .	287.0
1978	Edgar Van Wyck, Roland, Man .	382.0
1979	Howard Dill, Windsor, N. S .	438.5
1980	Howard Dill, Windsor, N. S .	459.0
1981	Howard Dill, Windsor, N. S .	493.5
1982	Howard Dill, Windsor, N. S .	445.0
1983	Owen Woodman, Falmouth, N. S .	481.0
1984	Owen Woodman, Falmouth, N . S .	564.5
1985	Mike Hodgson, River Philip, N. S .	531.0
1986	Edgar Van Wyck, Roland, Man.	548.0
1987	Will Neily, Spa Springs, N.S.	587.5
1988	Keith Chappell, Upper Granville, N.S.	633.5
1989	Gordon Thomson, Hemmingford, Que .	755.0
1990	Darren Woodworth, Berwick, N. S .	658.0
1991	Mike MacDonald, Sherbrooke, Que .	717.5
1992	Mike Eaton, Richmond, ON	660.5
1993	Norm Craven, Stouffville, ON	836.0
1994	Herman Bax, Brockville, ON	990.0
1995	Lorraine Orr, Howick, PQ	887.0
1996	Bill Greer, Picton, ON	1,006.0

Bill Greer of Picton, Ont., set a new Canadian and Great Pumpkin
Commonwealth record in 1996 with his 1,006-pound pumpkin.
(Tim Canniff)

THE WORLD'S ALL-TIME HEAVIEST PUMPKINS
AS OF OCTOBER 15, 1996

	WGT	YEAR	GROWER	WEIGHOFF	ORG
1	1,061.0	1996	Nathan & Paula Zehr, Lowville, NY	Clarence	WPC
2	1,006.0	1996	Bill Greer, Picton, ON	Ottawa	GPC
3	990.0	1994	Herman Bax, Brockville, ON	Ottawa	GPC
4	968.0	1995	Paula Zehr, Lowville, NY	Lowville	IPA
5	945.5	1994	Barry Dejong, Brockville, ON	Ottawa	GPC
6	941.0	1996	Al Eaton, Richmond, ON	Ottawa	GPC
7	940.0	1996	Pete Geerts, Arkona, ON	Ottawa	GPC
8	939.0	1995	Geneva Emmons, Issaquah, WA	Clackamas	GPC
9	923.0	1994	Glen Brown, Bethel, MN	Anamosa	GPC
10	914.0	1994	Craig Weir, Salisbury, MA	Topsfield	GPC
11	897.5	1996	Jack LaRue, Tenino, WA	Carnation	GPC
12	897.0	1996	Paul McIntyre, Oxford Mills, ON	Ottawa	GPC
13	887.0	1995	Lorraine Orr, Howick, PQ	Ottawa	GPC
14	887.0	1996	Tony Ciliberto, Wilkes-Barre, PA	Altoona	GPC
15	884.0	1993	Don Black, Winthrop, NY	Windsor	GPC
16	884.0	1996	Bob Schlutt, Bridgman, MI	Canfield	GPC
17	875.0	1995	Jack LaRue, Tenino, WA	Half Moon Bay	Indep
18	866.0	1996	Kirk Mombert, Harrisburg, OR	Carnation	GPC
19	850.0	1995	Jack LaRue, Tenino, WA	Clackamas	GPC
20	846.5	1995	Lyle Richart, Vancouver, WA	Clackamas	GPC
21	845.5	1995	Tony Ciliberto, Wilkes-Barre, PA	Ottawa	GPC
22	841.0	1996	Bill Edwards, Marshall, MI	St. John's	GPC
23	839.0	1995	Pat Ruelle, Redway, CA	Nut Tree	GPC
24	836.0	1993	Norm Craven, Stouffville, ON	Port Elgin	WPC
25	833.5	1995	Kirk Mombert, Harrisburg, OR	Clackamas	GPC

INDEP — INDEPENDENT

Rubber reptile ruptured in Dill pumpkin patch
by Glen Parker

WINDSOR—Howard Dill is famous for his giant 600-pound pumpkins. But the College Road farmer is gaining a sort of cult following for having his fake snake shot in one of his pumpkin patches.

"It was a blow-up, illustrated snake designed to scare off birds or animals that could hamper the growth of the plants," explained Howard. "You see them advertised in gardening magazines all the time." The fake snake measured about five feet long and, according to Howard, was "very real looking. In fact, it often scared me... you know, when you are working late in the evening in the pun'kin patch and you come across it when you're not expecting it!"

That is exactly what happened to Howard's neighbour,

Sally Fergusson. "We'd been away for the day and when we got home, I noticed our pony was loose and was standing in Howie's pumpkin patch," she recalled. It was late summer, and the pumpkins were starting to get pretty big. So Sally got the pony back and felt she should make sure the beast hadn't squashed her neighbour's cucerbitaceous plants.

"My God! I saw the snake," said Sally. "It was a large snake, seven or eight feet long with a diamond pattern on its back." Scared silly, Sally called her husband who arrived on the scene to declare the snake a "diamond-backed rattler."

"He even saw it move," recalled Sally. "I got the kids in the house and left orders with my husband not to let the snake out of his sight. I figured if it got away into the corn field we wouldn't be able to come out of the house again," she said. Sally then proceeded to call the local Department of Lands and Forests office. "It was (Hants County) Exhibition time and I figured the snake had escaped from a wildlife show that was part of the entertainment over there."

The Lands and Forests officer (who wishes to remain anonymous) remembered the incident very well. "First I drove a piece of mud at the snake," he said. "They wanted it shot so I up and let 'er have it!" Eyewitnesses reported the force of the shotgun blast hurled the snake 10 feet into the air. "There were bits of plastic everywhere, then we heard this w-o-o-o-s-h sound and the thing started darting all over the place," said Sally. "We just looked at each other and then broke up laughing when we realized that it was a plastic snake."

"Oh I knew it wasn't real," claimed the red-faced Lands and Forests officer. "Afterwards I said they'd be better off not telling anyone about this thing before word got around —you know, leave well enough alone!" Because of the concern the fake snake caused his good neighbours, Howard Dill did not seek remuneration.

Reprinted from the *Hants Journal.*

Favourite Recipes

Old-fashioned Pumpkin Pie

The following recipe comes from Hilda Dill, Howard's wife.
2 large eggs
2 cups cooked, mashed pumpkin
1 cup brown sugar
1/2 tsp. salt
1 tsp. cinnamon
1 tsp. nutmeg
1/4 tsp. ginger
1/2 tsp. mace
1-2/3 cups light cream
 Heat oven to 425° F. Prepare a 9-inch pie shell
(unbaked). Beat eggs slightly, add remaining ingredients.
Pour into pie shell. Bake 15 minutes at 425° then reduce heat
to 350°. Bake until knife inserted in centre comes out clean.
It takes a good hour to bake. With pumpkin pie, you use your
own favorite spices.

Pumpkin Cake

*You can, if you wish, replace the tablespoon of orange juice in the
filling with the same amount of Cointreau.*
3 eggs
1 cup sugar
3/4 cup cooked, mashed pumpkin
1 tbsp. lemon juice
3/4 cup all-purpose flour
1 heaped tsp. baking powder
1 tsp. each cinnamon, nutmeg
1/2 tsp. ginger
8 oz. cream cheese

1 tbsp. butter
1tbsp. undiluted frozen orange juice
1 cup powdered sugar
2 tbsp. liquid honey
1 cup chopped pecans

In medium bowl, beat eggs until frothy and lemon colored. Gradually add sugar, beating until mixture is slightly thickened. Add the pumpkin and lemon juice and mix until well blended. In another bowl, combine flour, baking powder and spices. Add to pumpkin mixture and beat until the flour disappears. Grease a 10 x 15 x l-inch baking pan and sprinkle with flour. Pour in batter and bake in a 375°F. oven for 12-15 minutes, or until a toothpick inserted comes out clean. Turn out onto a tea towel sprinkled with powdered sugar, and starting at the narrow end, roll up towel and cake together. Lay, seam-side down, on rack to cool. Meanwhile, blend together butter, cream cheese and orange. Add sugar, beating until smooth. Unroll the cooled cake, spread with filling and reroll. Wrap firmly in aluminum foil and refrigerate for at least three hours. Unwrap, brush with honey (if you warm the honey, it will be easier to spread) and roll in chopped nuts. Yields about 10 slices.

THE AUTHOR

Al Kingsbury was born in Sydney, N.S., where he graduated from Sydney Academy and began his newspaper career with *The Cape Breton Post*. After completing apprenticeship training as a compositor, he moved to Halifax and joined the staff of The Halifax Herald Limited in 1962.

He transferred to the Editorial Department of *The Chronicle-Herald* in 1980 and was named chief of the paper's Valley Bureau, with responsibility for all news gathering and features in the Annapolis Valley. He has done public relations work and compiled history books for United Memorial Church and Halifax Typographical Union, which he also served as secretary-treasurer and president.

He has worked on organizing committees of the Annapolis Valley Apple Blossom Festival since 1981 and served two terms as president. He represented Nova Scotia on the board of directors of the Canadian Association of Festivals and Events for two years. He is a member of the board of directors of Valley Regional Hospital Foundation and was chairman of its Equipment Fund Campaign.

He lives in Kentville with his wife Betty, the former Betty Cooper. They have two sons, a daughter and four grandchildren.